> *"Be who God meant you to be and you will set the world on fire."* —Saint Catherine of Siena

for tween/teen girls

BLAZE Core

A 20-lesson program that includes Truth vs. Lie Cards, a Prayer Journal, fun take-home gifts, and a Leader's Guide for an adult leader.

Discovering My Purpose

A six-lesson Bible study that will help you discover your spiritual gifts!

Between You and Me

A 40-day conversation guide for mothers and daughters.

walking with purpose

Learn more at walkingwithpurpose.com/BLAZE

Discovering My Purpose
Bible Study

Authored by Lisa Brenninkmeyer
Published by Walking with Purpose, Inc,

The recommended Bible translations for use in Walking with Purpose studies
are: The New American Bible, which is the translation used in the United States
for the readings at Mass; The Revised Standard Version, Catholic Edition; and
The Jerusalem Bible.

Cover and page design by Aliza Latta.

21 22 23 24 25 / 10 9 8 7 6 5 4

ISBN: 978-1-943173-21-1

Discovering My Purpose Bible Study

Printed in the United States of America

Be who GOD
meant you
to be
and you will
set the world
on fire.

ST. CATHERINE of SIENA

blaze

TABLE OF CONTENTS

INTRODUCTION

SESSIONS

APPENDICES

ANSWER KEY

What Is the Purpose of My Life?

God is seeking you out. And what He wants to show you is your part in His story—the grand story He's been writing since the beginning of time. I say *His* story because ultimately it is all about Him. When we make our lives all about us, we miss the point. We end up being motivated by making sure we get noticed, that people appreciate us, and that we get ahead. What's the result of this kind of life? We feel unfulfilled. We experience discontent.

In Hebrews 12:1–2, we are encouraged to "persevere in running the race that lies before us, while keeping our eyes fixed on Jesus." What is the result of keeping our eyes fixed on Jesus, on *His* story, *His* plan, *His* glory? It's a life of fulfillment and deep satisfaction. When He is the focus, there is no limit to the good He can do through us. When our ultimate goal is for Jesus to shine brightly in our world, we live differently. We dream big dreams. We are bold in our hopes. We take risks and really start living.

Sessions

NOTES

Session 1

THE PURPOSE WE ALL SHARE

1. Read Philippians 3:7–11. Saint Paul wrote these verses after listing all the impressive credentials and honors that he'd earned. He considered them all worthless ("I have come to consider everything a loss"), because of what higher good?

St. Paul said nothing was more important than knowing Jesus. No award, no athletic achievement, and no personal accomplishment would ever compare to that. No amount of popularity would ever come close to satisfying him the way that knowing Jesus did.

2. Read 2 Corinthians 5:18–19.

   A. What ministry has God given us and what message has He entrusted to us?

   The Message translation of the Bible explains it this way:

   > All this comes from the God who settled the relationship between us and him, and then called us to settle our relationships with each other. God put the world square with himself through the Messiah, giving the world a fresh start by offering forgiveness of sins. God has given us the task of telling everyone what he is doing.

   B. *Reconciliation* is the word used to describe dropping our differences and learning how to live and work together. It requires forgiveness, because if we hang on to our anger and bitterness, we won't ever be able to repair what's wrong in our relationships. This is exactly what Jesus did for us—He opened the way for us to have a close relationship with our heavenly Father. He now asks us to help reconcile others with Him and with each other. This is one of our core purposes in life. Are there any relationships in your life in which God is asking you to be a peacemaker?

3. Read 2 Corinthians 5:20. How are we described in this verse? In order to be true to this description, how should we interact with others?

Get quiet and go a little deeper. . . . The more you know Him, the more you'll love Him.

Nothing was more important to Saint Paul than knowing Christ. Every morning, he decided that he wanted to know Jesus better by that evening. As he came to know Jesus more and more, he made it his goal to show the world what Jesus is like by loving like He does. This is God's main purpose for you as well—to experience His love and to love others as He does.

To do this requires a choice. Imagine if a runner took her eyes off of the path ahead of her and kept turning and looking at things beside or behind her. She would be slowed down. She might lose sight of her end goal. She would likely fall. The same is true for us. If we want to live Jesus' purpose for our lives, we have to keep Him as our focus. We have to recognize that things like popularity, good grades, and athletic trophies might make us happy on some level, but making these things the center of our lives keeps us from running the race set before us. If they are our focus, we will be distracted from our end goal. And if we fail to make knowing Jesus and becoming more like Him our highest priority, we will have settled for a lesser, shallow existence.

Take some time to think about the things that tempt you to take your eyes off your primary purpose (knowing and becoming more like Jesus). Is it your reputation? Is it how many friends you have or how many boys want to date you? Your desire for comfort? Fear of being different? Ask God to help you put knowing Him and becoming more like Him ahead of all other goals.

NOTES

NOTES

Session 2

YOUR UNIQUE PURPOSE

Have you ever wondered if God has a specific plan for your life? Have you ever feared that He is too busy with bigger things to have time to think about you that much? I promise you, His love for you is personal and individual. Your heavenly Father doesn't just look on people in general; *He sees you*—you in all your uniqueness, you with your specific dreams, you with your fears and insecurities. He sees it all and He adores you. And He knows how He wants your life to turn out.

God wants you to make the focus of your life knowing and becoming more like Jesus. But He also wants you to know that you are unrepeatable and that He created you with something specific to offer the world. There is a difference that He wants you to make. There's a lot of suffering going on in people's lives and hearts, and He wants all of His children, with their own unique gifts, to go out into the world and help others.

God has given you a specific life purpose. This is something more unique to you than the general purpose we all share—knowing and becoming more like Jesus. This is something He created for you to do, and we're going to call it a "calling" or a "life purpose." When God gave out callings and life purposes, *He did not skip you*. God has a plan for your heart, for your life.

1. What phrases do you find in Psalm 139:13–16 that talk about how God created you?

When God formed you, He formed you with a specific purpose in mind. He had a plan for your life, even before you were born. That plan is not something to be afraid of; it is *good*. God reminded us of this in Jeremiah 29:11 when He said, "For I know the plans I have in mind for you, says the LORD, plans for your welfare, not for woe! Plans to give you a future full of hope!"

2. You might be thinking, "I believe that God has a plan for me, but how do I know what it is?" One of the ways that God reveals His specific plan for you is by giving you spiritual gifts. Spiritual gifts (also called charisms) are given to children of God to help them achieve the purpose they were created for. Read 1 Corinthians 12:1–11 and answer the following questions about spiritual gifts.

   A. Does God want you to be ignorant of your spiritual gifts? See 1 Corinthians 12:1.

   B. Is the same spiritual gift given to everyone? See 1 Corinthians 12:4–6.

   C. Who is the source of all spiritual gifts? See 1 Corinthians 12:6

   D. Who receives the manifestation (or gifts) of the Spirit? See 1 Corinthians 12:7.

   E. Do you get to choose your spiritual gifts? See 1 Corinthians 12:11.

One of the reasons it's important for us to realize that God gives us our spiritual gifts and chooses them for us is because we are so prone to compare ourselves to each other. Have you ever looked at another girl and wished that your abilities were more like hers? When we compare ourselves to others, it not only kills friendship, but it makes us feel insecure and unhappy. God doesn't want you to compare yourself to other girls; He wants you to discover and get excited about the spiritual gifts He's given to *you*. So we don't ask *for* a specific spiritual gift—we ask *to become aware* of which spiritual gift or gifts we've been given.

3. We saw in 1 Corinthians 12:8—10 that some of the spiritual gifts are wisdom, knowledge, faith, healing, prophecy, discernment of spirits, and tongues. What are some other spiritual gifts listed in Romans 12:6–8?

There are tons of different spiritual gifts, and each child of God has at least one. You were not skipped over when God was giving them out spiritual gifts. But it takes a little while sometimes to figure out which one He chose specifically for you.

Here's a list of some of them:

Exhortation (being able to encourage a friend to do the right thing in a way that isn't annoying)

Leadership (being able to get a group of people to work well together well towards a common goal)

Mercy (seeing the needs of others and going out and doing something to help)

Teaching (being able to explain things so that others can learn)

Administration (being good at details, able to get things done in an organized way)

Hospitality (making people feel welcome and like they belong)

Music (having a musical gift that leads other people to want to pray and grow closer to God)

Get quiet and go a little deeper. . . . God is so excited about the way He made you.

"For we are His handiwork, created in Christ Jesus for the good works that God has prepared in advance, that we should live in them." (Ephesians 2:10)

God created you—you are His handiwork, His masterpiece. *He didn't make you to sit still and look pretty. He made you and placed spiritual gifts inside you so that you would go out and make a difference in the world.*

What would change if we lived like we really believed that? Instead of spending all day thinking about who we are not and what we don't have, we could be world changers. It's time to let the truth of Ephesians 2:10 sink in—that we are God's masterpieces, His handiwork. He has created us to make a difference; He's placed unique gifts into each of us, and He wants us to use those gifts to help those around us. It's time to stop comparing and start serving.

We start to learn which spiritual gift we've been given by doing. *We step out and get involved in situations where we are going to need to rely on God to help us. Volunteering at school, at church, and in your community will give you ideas about where you enjoy serving and what you are good at. Both those things matter.*

What is holding you back? Are you waiting to see what the kids in your class will think if you start living like this? Are you waiting until you're an adult before you start making a difference? You don't need to wait for either of those things. God offers you courage and strength. He has got your back. Step out. *You don't have to be anyone other than the girl God created you to be. You are unique and gifted, and there's a world out there that needs you.*

This is a great time to take the Spiritual Gifts Assessment and read about the various gifts! You'll find this in Appendix 2.

NOTES

NOTES

Session 3

HOW TO DISCOVER YOUR UNIQUE PURPOSE

If you're going to live your life saying yes to God, you'll need to be brave. Most people around you are going to make decisions that are different from yours. That's because unless we decide that we don't care what others think, unless we care more what God thinks than what anyone else thinks, we're going to live pretty selfishly. Without God, we pretty much come to any situation trying to figure out the best way to get things to work in our favor. What will cause *me* to be noticed? How can *I* get ahead? What will feel good to *me*? But when we decide to live life like Jesus did, everything changes. We are different. And that can be hard and doesn't always feel good.

But one day, after we die, we'll be standing in front of God. I know that seems so far away . . . maybe it seems like it will never happen. But the truth is, one day we'll have to explain to God what we've done with the time, spiritual gifts, and other abilities He gave to us. I don't know about you, but I don't want to tell Him, "I stayed as comfortable as I could. I played it safe. I made sure that people liked me as much and as often as possible. I made sure that things worked out for me."

Instead, I want to tell Him that I went *all out*. I want to tell Him I gave it all I had, that sometimes helping other people made me really tired, but that He was worth every bit of what I sacrificed. How about you?

1. What types of service energize you? Can you think of a time when you've helped another person and received positive feedback about the results? Maybe you helped someone with her homework, or organized something for your mom, or got a group to work together. Maybe you enjoyed feeding the homeless. Have you sung in a choir for Mass? All those are ways that you can serve.

2. Every day, many people tell us what we should do and who we should be. Your friends tell you that there are certain things they think are really important for you to know about and be able to do. Your parents may want you to have certain hobbies or play certain sports. Kids at school may value something else, and you might feel that if you don't succeed in that area, you're worthless. We could spend our whole lives trying to please the people around us, but if we did, we might never figure out what God wants from us. To hear His voice, we have to set aside time to be quiet with Him in prayer. When we learn to hear His voice, the voices of everyone else around us start to be quieted.

A. What are some of the things you feel like people in your life expect you to do?

B. Do any of these things make it hard for you to make God the highest priority in your life?

C. What are some things that you know God wants you to do (like being honest, obeying Him, praying)?

D. Write out Galatians 1:10 in the space below.

This verse challenges us *not* to make being popular our highest goal. Instead, it tells us to make serving Jesus the most important thing. Sometimes obeying Jesus and doing what people want us to do are the same thing. It's always nice when it works out like that. But sometimes we have to make a choice between the two. When we face those choices, we should choose God. It may mean that we feel alone or uncomfortable right then. But in the long run, it will pay off. We'll become stronger and braver.

And sometimes, it is precisely in those difficult times, those times of loneliness and struggle, that God shows us the purpose He has for us. Saint Padre Pio says it this way: "The storms that are raging around you will turn out to be for God's glory, your own merit, and the good of many souls."

3. Thinking about difficult things that you've gone through can help you discover where God wants you to help in the world. Have you experienced something hard, like your parents' divorce? Do you find it difficult to discover your place and feel important in your family? Are you struggling with your grades at school? Do you find it tough to fit in at school? All those things are really tough, and can make us wonder why God doesn't just make things easier. I can't tell you why He allowed those things to happen, but I can promise you something: You are uniquely qualified to help another girl who is going through the same thing. Your understanding, comfort, and words will mean more because you have walked through the same circumstances she has. When we suffer, God offers us comfort and encouragement. What does He want us to do with the compassion and encouragement He has given us in our times of difficulty? See 2 Corinthians 1:3–4.

4. What suffering in the world (and it doesn't have to be far away—it might be in your neighborhood, your classroom, or your family) really troubles you? What gets you upset enough that you inwardly say, "Something has got to be done about this"?

Get quiet and go a little deeper. . . . Courageously dream with God about how you can make a difference in the world.

There isn't a simple formula to discover what God wants you to do in the world. You discover it over time by trying out different ways of serving, messing up a lot, and praying even more. Tell God about the things you see in the world that you think should change. Ask Him to take the things that you have found really hard in your life and use them to help someone else. Ask Him to show you what you are good at, and then promise Him that you'll use your gifts for the things that matter to Him instead of to bring attention to yourself.

NOTES

Session 4

YOU GET TO DECIDE

God created you with a particular purpose. He identified specific "works" (things that need to be done to help our hurting world) and He put your name on them. He sees all the things in the world that aren't right, and He wants you to do something about it. He gave you spiritual gifts so you could step out and make a difference. But He won't make you accept the call. He gives you free will. You get to decide what you're going to do with what He's given you and shown you.

1. When we discover our spiritual gifts (charisms), it can be tempting to use them to benefit ourselves. But who should ultimately benefit from spiritual gifts? See CCC 799 and 800.

"It is a wake-up call, a reminder that we are here for just a moment. How we spend that moment has eternal significance. Wanting more out of life is not about a desire to bring more attention to you. It's about wanting to find a way to do more with your life in a form of worship that ultimately brings more glory to God." —Jennie Allen

2. If we're going to fulfill our unique purpose while being an ambassador for Christ (showing others what He is like), what will our attitude need to be? See Matthew 20:26–28.

3. We are supposed to use our spiritual gifts to benefit others and bring glory to God, and we have to have a humble servant's attitude in order to do it well. So how come so few of us do it? Read John 12:24–25 to see why we find it so hard.

4. Why do you think we are so much more likely to do things not for the sake of others, but so that *we* get noticed?

Saying yes to God—serving so that He is noticed and not just so that we gain—doesn't feel very good in the moment. Do you want everyont to approve of you? You have to let that go, because I promise you that doing what God asks of you will mean someone in your life will disapprove of your choice. It's hard to care more about what God thinks than about what our friends think. Really hard. So I encourage you to ask God to help you want His approval more than anything.

Another thing—don't waste time saying, "I'm just not sure exactly what God wants me to do. So I'll just sit here and wait until it all becomes clear." Just step out and serve. Saint Teresa of Calcutta once said, "Never worry about numbers. Help one person at a time and always start with the person nearest you." In other words, meet the need that's right in front of you, without overanalyzing things or worrying that you won't be able to do enough. When you start to do this more, you'll begin to discover your "sweet spot"—that place where your passion and compassion meet. So what if some of the ways you've served turned out to be a little disastrous? God sees the intention in your heart. He sees the love that motivated you. Regardless of how it all turns out, you've chosen to step out in love. And that's what God wants to see.

Get quiet and go a little deeper. . . . Let Him change your perspective.

Dear Lord,

If I start to feel that what I can do doesn't make much of a difference, if I start comparing myself to people who seem to have way more abilities than I do, help me to remember that I am significant in Your eyes. You see the smallest act of love and it matters. Help me to remember that I'm not valued because of my gifts and talents. That is simply what You pour into me so that I can get out in the world and love people the way You love them. I'm valued because You made me; I'm Your beloved daughter, and You don't create mistakes.

On the other hand, if I start to get a little impressed with all that I'm doing, the difference I'm making, and the way people around me are thinking I'm pretty amazing, help me to remember that any good in me comes from You. May everything I do bring attention to You, not to me.

NOTES

Session 5

REAL-LIFE STORY: SAINT ROSE PHILIPPINE DUCHESNE

God's love is not generic. The Church teaches us that every single human being is created directly by God and every human being has a unique relationship with Him. We each know and love Him as *only we can*. This is why everyone's calling in life is specific.

We see this truth revealed to us through the lives of the saints. Some saints were rich; some were poor. Some grew up in incredible Catholic families; others were raised by pagans. Among the saints, we see missionaries, writers, doctors, scientists, soldiers, teachers, priests, religious, married people, and children. The uniqueness of each saint's life shows how God creates and calls each of us in a unique way.

Saint Rose Philippine Duchesne (1769–1852) came from a wealthy French family and had everything going for her. As a girl, she learned how to use her energetic and outgoing personality for all kinds of good deeds: visiting the sick and poor, giving alms, playing school. When the French Revolution broke out, she ministered to prisoners waiting to be executed; she gathered up orphans, taking care of them and teaching them the *Catechism*.

When she was only eight years old, she heard a homily by a priest who had recently been working in the French missions in America. From that moment on, her deepest desire was to become a missionary herself, and to minister to the Native Americans. More than sixty years would pass before that calling would be fulfilled.

At twelve, she told her father that she wanted to join a convent and dedicate her entire life to serving the Sacred Heart. Her father would hear none of it. But she persisted, and in the end she won. Her first obstacle was overcome. The rest of her life would be a series of increasingly larger obstacles, all of them overcome by her huge faith and especially her sheer determination. This determination did not come from her; it came from the word God had spoken in her heart when she was just a child.

During the French Revolution, the rebels had closed all religious houses. When the rebellion ended, Rose tried to restart her convent, but failed. So she invited another religious order to come take it over. After maturing in her own religious training, she and a couple of other nuns set out for America, where she still longed to be a missionary among the Native Americans. She was forty-nine years old. She fell ill on the trip across the Atlantic and almost died before reaching Louisiana. She fell ill again on the trip up the Mississippi, knocking on death's door for the second time.

When Rose finally reached her mission station, in Saint Charles, Missouri, she faced more difficult circumstances. Instead of getting to work with the population she was passionate about, the Native Americans, she had to begin her work with the white settlers—schools (including the first free school west of the Mississippi) and orphanages, along with the convents needed to train sisters to run them. She did her best to reach out to the Native Americans in her free time, but she only began working with them full-time when she turned seventy-one and was relieved of some of her administrative duties.

Throughout her years in America she suffered every kind of hardship and difficulty—famine, floods, poverty, sickness, the crudeness of paganism (the Native Americans used to bring her fresh scalps as a sign of their reverence)—but her prayer and willpower endured them all, and her missionary activity sowed the seeds of the Catholic Church in the Midwest. Today Rose's name is the first inscribed on the Pioneer roll of fame in the Jefferson Memorial Building in Saint Louis.

God had given her a specific call—a personal word to her heart. Her hearing and following it, despite enormous obstacles, changed the world forever.

Do you feel like God is calling you to take action in response to a specific need you see in the world, in your community, in your group of friends, or in your family? If so, what is that action?

Have difficulties caused you to question whether your actions will actually change anything? How does the story of Saint Rose Philippine inspire you to persevere?

NOTES

NOTES

Session 6

CROSSING THE FINISH LINE

1. A. Read 2 Timothy 4:7–8. What is our life described as?

   B. If our lives are a race, what is the finish line? What awaits us there (2 Timothy 4:8)?

   C. In order to run this race, you will need to be focused, to always have the end goal in mind. Read 1 Timothy 6:11–12. What are we told to pursue?

While the majority of the world pursues other things—perfect bodies, popularity, money, success, fame—we are encouraged to pursue virtue, devotion, faith, love, patience, and gentleness so as to live out God's pursuit for us.

2. To "compete well for the faith" (1 Timothy 6:12) and to live out the purpose God has created us for, we must keep our eyes on the end goal, eternal life. But if we are honest, so many things throughout the day cause us to lose focus on that end goal. What are those things for you? Is it the busyness of your schedule? Is it drama among the kids in your class? Is it that you focus too much on sports, music, social media? Is it other people's opinions of you? Write those things below.

God wants us to live with our eyes on heaven—with our focus on the day when we'll meet Him face-to-face. He wants us to long for the day when the race will be over and we will see Him, the just judge, and experience the reward of eternal life.

But He also wants you to use your time here on earth with purpose. He created you for a reason, and He doesn't want you to miss it. One of the reasons this is important to Him is because He has work that needs to be done in the world—suffering that needs to be relieved, comfort that needs to be given, teaching that needs to be heard, beauty that needs to be created—and He wants to do these things through His people. He wants to use you to fulfill His plan. Another reason this is so important to Him is that *He adores you*, and He wants you to experience the fulfillment and joy that come from being a part of His story and running the race He created you for. This is *your* race—not your sister's, or your mother's, or your friend's. *Yours.* Don't let yourself be distracted from running this race of yours.

3. What is one thing that you have learned about God's purpose for you during this study?

4. What is one thing that this study taught you about God's heart, about His love for you?

Get quiet and go a little deeper. . . . Remember, you are needed.

This life is full of distractions and temptations that try to keep us from focusing on our end goal. Run your race with your eyes fixed on the finish line, when you'll crash into God's arms, fully known and fully loved. Please don't give up and just settle for being comfortable. And please don't sit on your gifts and your calling because you are afraid that if you step out, you'll be criticized or you'll be too much or not enough. Rise up and take your place within God's story. You are needed. Run your race—the race you were created for. Don't miss it. Every moment of your life has meaning. You matter. What you offer the world matters. Take some time to reflect on this and to thank God for creating you with uniqueness and for a specific purpose.

My Resolution

In what specific way will I apply what I have learned in this Bible study?

Examples:

1. I'm going to set aside fifteen minutes each day for prayer so I can learn to hear God's voice.

2. I'm going to ask God to show me the ways that I focus on other people's approval instead of His.

3. I'm going to write down Psalm 139:14 ("I praise you, so wonderfully you made me") and put it on my mirror so I can remember that God created me uniquely, for a specific purpose.

My resolution:

Catechism Clips

CCC 799 Whether extraordinary or simple and humble, charisms are graces of the Holy Spirit which directly or indirectly benefit the Church, ordered as they are to her building up, to the good of men, and to the needs of the world.

CCC 800 Charisms are to be accepted with gratitude by the person who receives them and by all members of the Church as well. They are a wonderfully rich grace for the apostolic vitality and for the holiness of the entire Body of Christ, provided they really are genuine gifts of the Holy Spirit and are used in full conformity with authentic promptings of this same Spirit, that is, in keeping with charity, the true measure of all charisms.

NOTES

Appendices

NOTES

Appendix 1

SAINT TERESA OF CALCUTTA
PATRON SAINT OF BLAZE

Saint Teresa of Calcutta, more commonly known as Mother Teresa of Calcutta, was gifted with a heart to love the poorest of the poor. This blessed saint responded boldly to the call God had placed within her. She said yes to God with her whole heart, and because of her willingness to do so, she lived out her God-given purpose, became who she had been created to be, and set the world on fire. Saint Teresa is one of the greatest saints of our time because she was willing to turn away from the lie that the way she wanted to serve the people of Calcutta was impossible; instead, she wholeheartedly turned toward the truth that God would give her the strength to accomplish whatever He was calling her to do. When she turned to God and embraced this truth, her love was multiplied and the entire world was impacted by it.

Blaze is intended to be a program that ignites the hearts of middle school girls and provides them with the tools they need to cast off the lies of the world and instead fix their eyes on the truth that Christ reveals. It endeavors to teach girls how to hear the call God is placing on their hearts, and it is meant to challenge them to respond to that call with boldness, love, and faith. It is our hope that the girls will recognize that despite their young age, they, too, can set the world on fire when they become who they are meant to be.

Sometimes we think that to be a saint we need to do something extraordinary, something superhuman, something miraculous. Saint Teresa of Calcutta proves that this is not the case. In fact, her call wasn't all that special. God didn't call her to end world hunger or eradicate all violence. He called her to do little things with great love. Her call was simply to love, right where she was. And that is exactly what she did. Mother Teresa humbly loved the poor of India with everything she had, and the ripples of her impact reached around the globe. God took one woman's brave yes and changed the world. Blaze is intended to inspire girls to offer their own yes, right where they are planted. Just imagine what God can do through a generation of girls who know they are His beloved and bravely carry that message of hope to others.

Mother Teresa lived the gospel of love. In her own words, "We do not need to carry out grand things in order to show a great love for God and for our neighbor. It is the intensity of love we put into our gestures that makes them into something beautiful for God."[1]

Similarly, the challenges placed before middle school girls in Blaze are not huge. We are not asking them to give up everything they own for the poor or to run off and join a convent tomorrow. Instead, through this use of truths and lies, we are encouraging them to take a look at which lies have begun to take root in their hearts and to replace them with the life-giving truths of Jesus Christ. The changes are small, but when done with love, they can be astoundingly transformative.

Mother Teresa changed the world because she knew, deep in her soul, that her true identity was as a beloved daughter of God. She spent her life being filled up by divine love, and then allowing it to flow into the lives of others. Mother Teresa altered people's lives because she treated others like the beloved sons and daughters they were.

Our hope is that Blaze will help middle school girls begin to identify as the beloved and learn how they are called to love others like the beloved. We believe that if they do this, through the intercession of Saint Teresa of Calcutta, they, too, will set the world ablaze.

---

[1] Mother Teresa, *No Greater Love* (New York: MJF Books, 1997), 26.

Appendix 2

BLAZE SPIRITUAL GIFTS ASSESSMENT

Respond to each of the following statements with a number that shows how well the statement is true to *who you are*. This is not about how you wish you were or think you ought be. Do you think the statement describes you perfectly? Not at all? Or maybe somewhere in between? When you have read and ranked all of the statements, use the scorecard at the end to find out your results! God has certainly blessed you with at least one of the gifts listed at the end of this assessment. Let's find out how you can use your gifts to strengthen your relationships with Christ and with others, and to become who God made you to be!

RESPOND TO EACH STATEMENT USING THIS NUMBER SCALE

0 = Not at all, never, this does not sound like me
1 = Some of the time, once in a while, if someone encourages me to do this then I will
2 = Most of the time, usually true, this doesn't exactly describe me but it's close
3 = Consistently, definitely true, I feel comfortable doing this, this is definitely me

1. _____ I enjoy and am good at organizing people, tasks, and events.
2. _____ I enjoy using my artistic talents.
3. _____ I can easily tell whether someone is being genuine or fake.
4. _____ I like to talk to people when they are feeling down and help them to see their own potential.
5. _____ I truly believe that God has amazing plans for my life.
6. _____ I like when I find small, helpful tasks to accomplish without being asked and without anyone knowing that I did them.
7. _____ I like to help with social events at school or at Church.
8. _____ Whenever I or someone I know is having a difficult time, my first instinct is to pray about it.
9. _____ I am usually the one to speak up and take charge in a confusing situation.
10. _____ It is easy for me to see past people's faults or problems and treat them like God's beloved child.
11. _____ Listening to Christian music always makes me feel happy.
12. _____ Usually, people understand better when I explain something to them.
13. _____ I most enjoy expressing my love for God by writing journals, prayers, or poems.
14. _____ I like to plan each step out before I begin a project.

15. _____ I enjoy making the gifts that I give to others instead of buying them.

16. _____ I can tell if something is right or wrong, good or evil, true or a lie.

17. _____ I like to use my words to comfort or encourage others.

18. _____ People tell me that my hope in God, even during difficult situations, inspires them.

19. _____ When I do work, I don't care who gets the credit.

20. _____ I love to invite new people to hang out with my friend group.

21. _____ I love spending time with Jesus in prayer.

22. _____ I am usually the one who organizes and motivates everyone in group projects at school or church.

23. _____ I act from my feelings, not always logic.

24. _____ My favorite way to give thanks to God is to praise Him through singing, dancing, or playing music.

25. _____ I love learning new things and sharing what I've learned with others.

26. _____ Sometimes, people can understand something more clearly once they've read what I've written.

27. _____ I can distance myself from my feelings in order to make logical decisions.

28. _____ I like to work with my hands.

29. _____ I quickly understand whether someone's words contain God's truth or not.

30. _____ I have given hope to others by telling them about God's love and plans for them.

31. _____ I am confident that God is personally and deeply involved in my life.

32. _____ I like doing routine jobs like cleaning, yard work, and other small but important tasks, especially if it helps someone else do their own work.

33. _____ People often say that they feel at home with me or at my house.

34. _____ If someone asks me to pray for a special intention, I keep them in my prayers for many days.

35. _____ I like to be an example of how to live a Christian life by my actions.

36. _____ People have told me that I was a comfort to them when they were having a hard time.

37. _____ I prefer using my musical talents to sing, dance to, and play Christian music much more than secular music.

38. _____ I feel sure that the Holy Spirit has sometimes given me just the right words to explain something to another person.

39. _____ I love to write down Bible verses and what I have learned about them.

40. _____ In a group, I can easily see how everyone can contribute to complete a project.

41. _____ I like to glorify God through my artwork and the things I make.

42. _____ People often tell me that I am a good judge of character.

43. _____ I am not afraid to challenge someone if I know it will help them grow.

44. _____ I don't worry very much because I know that God is in control.
45. _____ I feel very connected to God when I am doing practical work around my school, house, church, or community.
46. _____ I like to go out of my way to make people feel comfortable and welcomed at school, in my church, and at home.
47. _____ People have told me that my prayers for them have been answered.
48. _____ People have told me that they look up to me.
49. _____ I am very patient with people because their struggles and hurts weigh on my heart.
50. _____ People have told me that my musical talents have helped them feel the joy of the Gospel.
51. _____ Education and learning are very important to me.
52. _____ Sometimes I feel the Holy Spirit giving me the right words to write.
53. _____ I can share my goals with others in a way that motivates them to help me.
54. _____ When I think about how I want to praise God, I first think about using my hands to make something.
55. _____ I can usually see something as sinful right away and avoid it.
56. _____ When I read the Bible, I like to look for practical advice for myself and others.
57. _____ I am absolutely sure that everything that happens in my life is according to God's plan and will be for my good.
58. _____ I would rather be working behind the scenes than leading the group.
59. _____ When I'm in a group of people, I am always looking to see if someone looks lonely or shy so that I can talk to them.
60. _____ Praying is easy and enjoyable for me.
61. _____ Other people are usually willing to follow my advice or listen to me when trying to solve a problem.
62. _____ I tend to find myself helping people who are "undeserving" or seemingly beyond anyone's help.
63. _____ I love to pray using music.
64. _____ I pay close attention to my teachers and how they explain confusing concepts to the class.
65. _____ I prefer to write my thoughts to God instead of speaking them out loud.

DIRECTIONS FOR SCORING

Enter the scores from each question in the corresponding numbered boxes (e.g. the score from question number 1 will go in the box labeled "1"). Add up each column and write the score in the box at the bottom, which is labeled with a letter. Each letter corresponds with a gift, listed below. The highest scores represent your gift or gifts! Continue reading for information, Bible passages, and saints that will help you learn more about who God made you to be.

1	2	3	4	5	6	7	8	9	10	11	12	13
14	15	16	17	18	19	20	21	22	23	24	25	26
27	28	29	30	31	32	33	34	35	36	37	38	39
40	41	42	43	44	45	46	47	48	49	50	51	52
53	54	55	56	57	58	59	60	61	62	63	64	65
A	B	C	D	E	F	G	H	I	J	K	L	M

A. Administration
B. Art
C. Discernment
D. Exhortation/Encouragement
E. Faith
F. Service/Helping
G. Hospitality
H. Intercession/Prayer
I. Leadership
J. Mercy/Compassion
K. Music
L. Teaching
M. Writing

ADMINISTRATION

"That you might set right what remains to be done . . ." Titus 1:5

If God has given you the gift of administration, then you are especially capable when serving through strategically organizing groups of people, events, tasks, and ministry goals. You are organized, humble, and intelligent.

How to use this gift: Volunteer to be on the leadership team for retreats and service trips; when working on group projects, help everyone find the job they would be best at; help to organize events at your school or church.

Ways this gift can be misused: When this gift is not paired with humility, it can be easy to forget to ask people for their opinions and instead to become controlling and closed off to other people's ideas.

Saint: Katharine Drexel

ART

"God looked at everything he made, and found it very good." Genesis 1:31

If God has given you the gift of being an artist, then you enjoy creating beautiful works of art that testify to God's love and beauty to anyone who views them. You are creative, perceptive, and inspiring.

How to use this gift: Create artwork for church events or advertisements for youth groups or Bible studies; share your faith by expressing God's love through a variety of artistic mediums; post your artwork on social media and talk about how your faith influences your art.

Ways this gift can be misused: When this gift is not paired with humility, it can be easy to become more interested in gaining recognition for your artwork than in the glory you can give to God.

Saint: Catherine of Bologna

DISCERNMENT
"Happy the one who finds wisdom, the one who gains understanding!" Proverbs 3:13

This gift allows the receiver to easily understand when a message is coming from God and is true, and when it is coming from Satan or from human pride. You are perceptive, intelligent, and trustworthy.

How to use this gift: You are able to determine whether advice should be followed or avoided, whether to believe something someone is saying, whether a teaching is rooted in the love of Christ or the sin of evil, whether someone is a fake or genuine friend.

Ways this gift can be misused: When this gift is not paired with humility, it is easy to begin to think that you are the authority on what is good and what is bad belief, friendship, or advice instead of recognizing that God is the source of all truth.

Saint: Elizabeth, cousin of Mary

EXHORTATION/ENCOURAGEMENT
"Therefore, encourage one another and build one another up . . ." 1 Thessalonians 5:11

If God has given you the gift of exhortation, sometimes also called encouragement, then you have a special ability to console others with words of comfort, hope, and affirmation when they are feeling especially discouraged. Exhortation also involves challenging people with hard advice when they are in need of guidance in their faith. You are well-spoken, perceptive, and kind.

How to use this gift: Remind a friend of God's love for them when they are having a difficult time; volunteer at nursing homes to talk with people who feel lonely; ask people how they are doing and really listen to how they are feeling.

Ways this gift can be misused: When this gift is not paired with humility, it can be easy to forget to really listen; you may care only about solving someone's problems instead of seeing them as a person who needs to be comforted and loved.

Saint: Maria Romero Meneses

FAITH

"Jesus said to them in reply, 'Have faith in God. Amen, I say to you, whoever says to this mountain, 'Be lifted up and thrown into the sea,' and does not doubt in his heart but believes that what he says will happen, it shall be done for him." Mark 11:22–23

If God has given you the gift of faith, then you are especially trusting in His plan for you, knowing without worry or doubt that He is always personally and intimately present in your life. You are trusting, confident, and courageous.

How to use this gift: When a friend is particularly worried about something, help her to see that God already knows what will happen and has her best interests in mind; live as an example of peacefulness in a world of stress and chaos; share your confidence in God, especially with people who feel like He has forgotten them.

Ways this gift can be misused: When this gift is not paired with humility, it can be easy to look down on others and view yourself as better because you know the love of Jesus and they doubt or are confused.

Saint: Thérèse of Lisieux

SERVICE/HELPING

"Bless the Lord, all you his hosts, his ministers who carry out his will." Psalm 104:21

If God has given you the gift of service, then you feel like you are doing Jesus' work on earth especially when you do routine and necessary behind-the-scenes jobs that enable others to live more comfortably and do their ministry. You are humble, hardworking, and generous.

How to use this gift: Volunteer in your community or on service trips; serve food at homeless shelters or soup kitchens; reach out to people who are having a hard time by offering to do practical jobs for them like cooking meals, cleaning, helping with homework, or babysitting.

Ways this gift can be misused: When this gift is not paired with humility, you can begin to decide for yourself what work needs to be done, without asking the person you are trying to help. This means that your focus is no longer on the other person but on how much work you can get done.

Saint: Azelie-Marie Martin

HOSPITALITY

"So he invited them in and showed them hospitality." Acts 10:23

If God has given you the gift of hospitality, then you are especially aware of people who might feel lonely or who look like they don't fit in, and you enjoy helping these people to feel welcome and comfortable. You are kind, perceptive, and gentle.

How to use this gift: Invite new people to hang out with your friend group; help anyone who looks like they are on the outside of a group and too shy to join in by asking them questions and getting them involved in the conversation; invite friends to church or youth group and introduce them to anyone they might not know.

Ways this gift can be misused: When this gift is not paired with humility, it can be easy to think about popularity and being likable instead of thinking about the person who is feeling left out or alone.

Saint: Martha

INTERCESSION/PRAYER

"With all prayer and supplication, pray at every opportunity in the spirit." Ephesians 6:18

If God has given you the gift of prayer, then you especially enjoy time spent with Jesus in prayer and feel like you have the right words to pray for the intentions of other people. You are trusting, generous, and intentional.

How to use this gift: Ask your friends what they are worried about and promise to pray for those worries every day for a week; pray out loud with your family before meals or at bedtime; start a group message on your phone with your friends so everyone can text their prayer intentions.

Ways this gift can be misused: When this gift is not paired with humility, it can be easy to try and make your prayers sound beautiful and eloquent and forget that you are in a relationship with Jesus in which He wants to hear you, but He also wants you to listen and be open to His words.

Saint: Teresa of Ávila

LEADERSHIP

"You will receive power when the Holy Spirit comes upon you, and you will be my witnesses . . . to the ends of the earth." Acts 1:8

If God has given you the gift of leadership, then you are especially able to serve through helping a group of people build relationships and motivating them to work together to reach a common goal. You are courageous, perceptive, and well-spoken.

How to use this gift: Start or lead a Bible study club after school; volunteer to lead a retreat, or a discussion group during youth group; take the initiative to include people who might usually be left out; let your actions be an example of kindness and faithfulness; post messages and images about your faith on social media.

Ways this gift can be misused: When this gift is not paired with humility, leaders can tend to strive for popularity or attention instead of using their gift to bring people together, to be a good example and role model, and to be a servant leader by working behind the scenes or taking the difficult steps to allow everyone else to feel included and cared for.

Saint: Joan of Arc

MERCY/COMPASSION

"Blessed are the merciful for they will be shown mercy." Matthew 5:7

If God has given you the gift of compassion, the hardships of the sick, lost, lonely, and abandoned weigh heavy on your heart, and you are especially drawn to helping the people who seem to be forgotten or have been given up on. You are kind, patient, and gentle.

How to use this gift: Volunteer in nursing homes or hospitals; go on a service trip to or volunteer around your community to help the poor; invite the person in your class who everyone seems to forget or tease to sit with you at lunch.

Ways this gift can be misused: When this gift is not paired with humility, you might have difficulty accepting the help others offer you because you see yourself not as someone who needs but as the person who has it all together in order to give to others.

Saint: Teresa of Calcutta

MUSIC
"Give praise with blasts upon the horn, praise him with harp and lyre. Give praise with tambourines and dance, praise him with strings and pipes. Give praise with crashing cymbals . . . Let everything that has breath give praise to the Lord." Psalm 150:3–6

If God has given you the gift of music, you especially enjoy praising Him through song, dance, or playing instruments, and through your musical abilities, you lead others to know His love. You are creative, courageous, and engaging.

How to use this gift: Sing or play an instrument with your church choir; post videos of you dancing to or singing Christian music; share with people how your music or dancing helps you to connect with Jesus in a special way.

Ways this gift can be misused: When this gift is not paired with humility, it can be easy to become more interested in gaining recognition for your talents than in the glory you can give to God.

Saint: Cecilia

TEACHING
"They taught in Judah, having with them the book of the Law of the Lord . . ." 2 Chronicles 17:9

If God has given you the gift of teaching, then you can easily comprehend and explain concepts in a way that enables others to understand and implement what they have learned. You are patient, intelligent, and well-spoken.

How to use this gift: Volunteer to tutor younger students either at your school or at a school in an impoverished area near you; help a friend who is struggling in school to study for a test or complete her homework; start a group message on your phone to prepare for a test and allow your friends to ask questions and help each other learn.

Ways this gift can be misused: When this gift is not paired with humility, it can be tempting to look down on the people you are helping because you can understand concepts that they are having difficulty with.

Saint: Elizabeth Ann Seton

WRITING

"We are writing this so that our journey may be complete." 1 John 1:4

If God has given you the gift of writing, then you can articulate difficult concepts and meaningful stories with clarity and beauty for others to read and be moved by. You are intelligent, creative, and perceptive.

How to use this gift: Write an article for your school's newspaper about your service trip or about something your church is doing in the community; write poems that will help others praise God; write a story about someone's faith journey; write social media posts advertising your youth group or Bible study.

Ways this gift can be misused: When this gift is not paired with humility, it can be easy to become more interested in gaining recognition for your writing than in the glory you can give to God.

Saint: Maria Faustina Kowalska

NOTES

Answer Key

NOTES

Session 1

1. Saint Paul considered all his worldly accolades worthless compared to the good of knowing Christ.
2. **A.** God has given each of us the ministry of reconciliation and the message of reconciliation.

   B. Answers will vary.
3. We are ambassadors for Christ, as if God were appealing through us. We are called to represent Christ to the world. If we are His ambassadors, we need to act as He would in all situations. He wants all our interactions with people to reflect His heart of mercy, kindness, and reconciliation. When we grow more and more like Jesus, allowing God to appeal to people through us, we're fulfilling our daily mission.

Session 2

1. God knit you together in your mother's womb, forming your inmost being. This is the part of you—your soul—that makes you unique. God's eyes have foreseen all your actions. He formed a plan for your life before you were born.
2. **A.** No. He doesn't want us to be unaware of our spiritual gifts.

   B. No, there are different kinds of spiritual gifts.

   C. The Holy Spirit is the source of the spiritual gifts; He distributes them individually as He wishes.

   D. Each individual receives the manifestation of the Spirit. This means that *no child of God* is skipped over.

   E. You don't get to choose your spiritual gifts. He decides what will best equip you for the mission He calls you to in life.
3. Romans 12:6–8 lists the following spiritual gifts: prophecy, ministering, teaching, exhortation, generosity, diligent leadership, and mercy. First Corinthians 12:8–10 lists the following spiritual gifts: wisdom, knowledge, faith, healing, mighty deeds, prophecy, discernment of spirits, varieties of tongues, and interpretation of tongues. Ephesians 4:11 lists the following spiritual gifts: apostleship, prophecy, evangelism, teaching, and pastoring.

Session 3

1. Answers will vary.
2. **A.** Answers will vary.

   B. Answers will vary.

   C. Answers will vary.

   D. "Am I now currying favor with human beings or God? Or am I seeking to please people? If I were still trying to please people, I would not be a slave of Christ." Galatians 1:10
3. We are to take the encouragement we received from God during our difficulties and then go to those who are hurting and offer them that same encouragement. Because we have *been there*, we are uniquely equipped to offer words of comfort and hope.
4. Answers will vary.

Session 4

1. Our spiritual gifts (charisms) have been given to us to benefit others. They are to be outwardly focused, used to build up the Church and meet the needs of the world. They should be exercised in charity; in other words, they should be used in a spirit of selfless love.

2. We begin with the attitude of a servant. We recognize that we've been given gifts for the benefit of others. We start at the bottom, serving humbly.

3. If we really want to see significant fruit come from our service, we are going to have to die to self, and that is really hard. It's a form of suffering, and we typically run from instead of toward suffering.

4. Answers will vary.

Session 6

1. **A.** Our life is described as a race.

   B. The Lord is waiting for you at the finish line with a crown of righteousness.

   C. We are to pursue righteousness, devotion, faith, love, patience, and gentleness.

2. Answers will vary.

3. Answers will vary.

4. Answers will vary.

NOTES

NOTES

NOTES

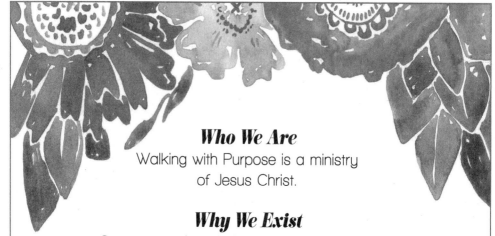

Who We Are
Walking with Purpose is a ministry
of Jesus Christ.

Why We Exist
Our purpose is to help women and girls know
Jesus Christ personally by making Scripture and the
teachings of the Catholic Church relevant and applicable.

Our Mission
Our mission is to help every Catholic woman and girl in
America encounter Jesus Christ through our Bible studies.

Our Vision
Our vision for the future is that, as more Catholic
women deepen their relationships with Jesus Christ,
eternity-changing transformation will take place in their
hearts – and, by extension – in their families, in their
communities, and ultimately, in our nation.

walking with purpose

You can support our mission through a tax-deductible gift.
Learn more at walkingwithpurpose.com/donate